THE ART OF TIME MANAGEMENT

How To Maximize Productivity
and Achieve Goals

Ray Goodwin

CONTENTS

Improvement

LIABILITY DISCLAIMER

The information contained within this book is intended for informational purposes only and should not be construed as legal or professional advice. The authors and publishers of this book are not responsible for any losses or damages that may arise from the use of the information contained within.

The reader assumes full responsibility for any decisions made based on the information in this book. The authors and publishers do not endorse any particular method, service or product mentioned in this book and are not responsible for any consequences resulting from their use.

The reader should exercise caution and discretion when making life changing decisions, and should be aware of the risks and potential consequences of their actions. This book is not a substitute for professional or legal advice and should not be relied upon as such.

By reading and using the information in this book, the reader acknowledges and agrees to hold harmless the authors, publishers, and any other parties involved in the creation or distribution of this book from any and all liability, claims, damages, or losses that may arise from their use of the information contained herein.

CHAPTER 1:
INTRODUCTION TO
TIME MANAGEMENT

Welcome to The Art of Time Management! In this book, we will explore the techniques and principles that successful people use to manage their time effectively. As an author with over 25 years of experience in online sales, I have learned firsthand the importance of managing one's time wisely in order to achieve success.

Time is a precious and finite resource. It's something that we can't control or create more of, but what we can do is learn how to maximize it. The ability to manage your time effectively can mean the difference between success and failure, both in your personal and professional life.

But effective time management is not just about cramming as much into each day as possible; it's about finding a balance between all areas of your life. In this book, I will guide you through the process of assessing your priorities, setting goals, creating schedules, and learning how to say "no" when necessary.

Throughout the pages of this book, you will discover tips and techniques for managing your time efficiently without sacrificing quality or burning yourself out. You will learn how to streamline your work processes and eliminate distractions so that you can focus on what truly matters.

So if you're ready to take control of your time and start achieving greater success in all areas of your life, then let's begin.

Overview

Time management is the art of maximizing the use of time in an efficient and effective manner. It involves the ability to prioritize tasks, plan ahead, and allocate time for activities that align with one's goals and priorities. In today's fast-paced world, time management has become a critical skill for personal and professional success.

Many people believe that time management is simply about making a schedule or using a planner. However, it goes beyond that. Effective time management requires self-awareness, discipline, and the ability to adapt to changing circumstances. It is a dynamic process that requires continuous improvement.

The benefits of effective time management are immense. It allows individuals to accomplish more in less time, reduce stress and improve overall well-being. Effective time management leads to increased productivity and helps individuals achieve their goals and aspirations. The ability to manage time effectively also showcases a person's professionalism and reliability to colleagues and superiors.

The connection between productivity and time management is undeniable. Productivity is about achieving maximum output with minimum input. Effective time management is one of the key components of achieving productivity. By managing time efficiently, one can increase focus and concentration, reduce distractions and interruptions, and increase creativity and innovation.

Procrastination is a common issue that affects time management. It is the act of delaying or postponing tasks that need to be done, especially when there is a looming deadline. Procrastination can have dire consequences on personal and professional life. It can lead to missed opportunities, mediocre performances, and mental exhaustion.

Poor time management can have a significant impact on personal and professional life. Prolonged periods of stress, burnout, and missed deadlines can lead to career setbacks, relationship issues, and mental health problems.

Setting realistic goals and expectations for time management is crucial. It is essential to recognize one's limitations and create a plan that is both achievable and effective. This requires planning, prioritizing, and assigning a period to carry out each task.

Throughout this book, we will explore different aspects of time management. We will start with understanding our personal time management style and assessing our current habits to improve upon. We will move on to creating a time management plan that works for us, explore tips on how to boost productivity and overcome procrastination, followed by eliminating time wasters, setting goals, and personal development.

In conclusion, mastering the art of time management can have a significant impact on personal and professional success. However, it is not an overnight process. It requires self-discipline, self-awareness, and a willingness to continuously learn and evolve. In the upcoming chapters, we will discuss how to effectively manage time in various scenarios like work-life balance, team management, and even retirement. By implementing personal time management techniques that work for you, you can ultimately achieve more and live a fulfilling life.

CHAPTER 2: UNDERSTANDING YOUR PERSONAL TIME MANAGEMENT STYLE

Time management is essential to success and personal growth. Understanding and working with your personal time management style is crucial to improve productivity and achieve your goals. Developing a solid understanding of your time management habits, strengths, and weaknesses, provides you with the knowledge and tools to create effective time management strategies tailored to your needs.

Different approaches to time management:

There are different approaches to time management, and each person has a unique way of managing time. Some people strictly follow a routine, while others rely on flexibility to manage their time. Understanding your approach to time management can help you develop personal strategies that enhance your productivity.

Assessing your current time management habits:

Begin by evaluating your current time management habits. How do you organize your day? How often do you check your emails or social media? Do you prefer to have a to-do list or simply keep everything in your head? By assessing your habits, you can identify areas where you excel or need improvement.

Identifying your strengths and weaknesses in time management:

Identifying your strengths and weaknesses in time management is key to understanding your personal time management style. Maybe you excel at prioritizing tasks but tend to get easily distracted by meetings or interruptions. Perhaps you have trouble setting and meeting deadlines but thrive when tackling new and exciting projects. Identifying your strengths and weaknesses allows you to focus on improving specific areas for enhanced productivity.

Tips for maximizing personal time management style:

Once you've identified your strengths and weaknesses, focus on improving specific areas. For example, if you tend to get easily distracted, create a schedule that includes time for focused work and limit interruptions when possible. If you struggle with procrastination or meeting deadlines, set clear goals and deadlines, and hold yourself accountable.

Developing new and effective time management strategies:

Developing new time management strategies to focus on your strengths and improve your weak areas is crucial. If you struggle with multitasking, try single-tasking by dedicating your focus on one task at a time. If a strict schedule doesn't work for you, try incorporating more flexibility in your day. Developing new strategies takes time, but experimenting and adjusting your approach can lead to improved productivity.

How to adapt your time management style to different situations:

Adapting your approach to time management to different situations is essential to success. For example, if you work in a fast-paced environment where the priorities shift constantly, flexibility is key. But if you have a lengthy project that requires close attention, it may be more effective to set and stick to a strict schedule. Learning to adapt your approach to time management not only helps you to maximize productivity but also helps you to navigate different situations with ease.

The importance of self-awareness in time management:

Self-awareness is crucial to effective time management. By recognizing what works for you and what doesn't, you can create personalized strategies that work best for you. Self-awareness also allows you to recognize when it's time to change your approach or ask for help.

Self-reflection exercises to improve time management skills:

Self-reflection exercises are key to improving time management skills. Evaluate your progress regularly and take note of what worked and what didn't. Reflect on how you spent your day and plan for improvements. Setting aside time for self-reflection can help you fine-tune your approach to time management and stay focused on your goals.

In conclusion, understanding your personal time management style is crucial to personal growth and productivity. By assessing your habits, identifying your strengths and weaknesses, and developing new strategies that work best for you, you can maximize your productivity and achieve your goals. Additionally, self-awareness and self-reflection exercises are important tools to improve and refine your time management habits for ongoing success.

CHAPTER 3: CREATING A TIME MANAGEMENT PLAN

Time is an unrenewable resource, and that is why it is imperative to create a plan that will help you manage it effectively. Having a time management plan can help you prioritize your tasks, increase productivity, and reduce stress. In this chapter, we will discuss how to create a time management plan that works for you.

The Importance of Planning in Time Management

Planning is a critical aspect of time management because it enables you to allocate your resources effectively. To create an effective plan, you need to understand your priorities, goals, and objectives. Without having a clear understanding of these things, it will be difficult to manage your time effectively.

Creating a Daily, Weekly, and Monthly Schedule

One of the fundamental principles of time management is creating a schedule. It will help you allocate time to accomplish tasks and prevent you from wasting time on less important things. There are different types of schedules that you can create, such as a daily, weekly, and monthly schedule.

A daily schedule is ideal for individuals who have a lot of tasks to accomplish in a day. It helps to ensure that you stay on track and manage your time effectively. A weekly schedule is suitable for people who have several tasks to complete within a week. It provides an overview of what needs to be done and helps you allocate time for tasks that require more time and energy.

A monthly schedule, on the other hand, is an excellent tool for individuals who have long-term goals they want to achieve. It provides an overview of the month, allows you to allocate time for tasks that require more time and energy, and helps you plan ahead.

Setting Priorities and Organizing Tasks

To create an effective time management plan, it is essential to set priorities and organize your tasks. Prioritization involves identifying the most important tasks and completing them first. When you organize your tasks, you understand the sequence of tasks that need to be completed to avoid wasting time jumping from task to task.

Establishing Clear Goals and Objectives

Setting goals and objectives is a fundamental principle of effective time management. Goals provide direction and help you visualize what you want to achieve. Objectives, on the other hand, are specific tasks that help you achieve your goals. When setting goals, ensure that they are SMART (Specific, Measurable, Achievable, Relevant, and Time-bound).

The Role of Flexibility in Time Management Planning

Flexibility is essential when creating a time management plan because it enables you to adapt to unexpected interruptions or changes. A plan that is too rigid may cause you to become overwhelmed, especially when unexpected events occur. Flexibility enables you to adjust your schedule and tasks to ensure that you remain productive, even when things do not go as planned.

Tips for Creating a Realistic Time Management Plan

Creating a realistic time management plan is crucial because it allows you to allocate resources effectively and avoid overcommitting yourself. To create a realistic plan, you need to understand your priorities, set achievable goals, organize your tasks, and be flexible.

Strategies for Dealing with Unexpected Interruptions and Distractions

Unexpected interruptions and distractions are common, and they can significantly impact your time management plan, resulting in low productivity. To deal with these distractions, you can create a buffer time in your schedule to accommodate unexpected events. You can also use tools such as noise-cancelling headphones to eliminate distractions and take breaks periodically to recharge.

Time Management Tools and Resources to Enhance Productivity

Several tools and resources can help you manage your time effectively. These include software, apps, and other resources. Some of the tools that can help you manage your time effectively include Trello, Asana, Google Calendar, and RescueTime. These tools can help you stay organized, increase productivity, and reduce stress.

In conclusion, creating a time management plan is fundamental to effective time management. It enables you to allocate your resources effectively, prioritize your tasks, and reduce stress. The key to creating an effective time management plan is to understand your priorities, organize your tasks, set achievable goals, and be flexible. Time management tools and resources are also essential in helping you manage your time effectively.

CHAPTER 4: TIME MANAGEMENT FOR PRODUCTIVITY

Time management is key to productivity. In today's fast-paced world, it is crucial to make the most of every minute. Many people often have a long to-do list but feel overwhelmed, not knowing where to start. In this chapter, we will discuss strategies for boosting productivity through effective time management.

1. Importance of setting deadlines and sticking to them

Setting deadlines is critical in achieving goals. Without time-bound targets, tasks can sprawl endlessly, draining time, and energy. Creating a timeline for every task and project helps to stay organized and focused. Determine the time needed for each activity and assign a time slot. Review the deadline regularly to make sure you are on track and adjust if necessary.

2. Delegating tasks to maximize productivity

Delegation is a critical skill for effective time management. Everyone has a limited amount of time and energy. By delegating certain tasks to others, you can focus on what you do best and maximize your productivity. However, delegation requires trusting others to complete the task satisfactorily. To ensure success, ensure that the team understands the project's objectives, responsibilities are clearly defined, and communication is regular.

3. Setting boundaries and managing expectations

Boundaries and expectations are essential for effective time management. Learning to say no is important when tasks are beyond their scope or capabilities. Saying yes to everything can leave one overwhelmed and unfocused. Managing expectations is equally important. Learn to communicate deadlines and schedules realistically to avoid overpromising and underdelivering.

4. Strategies for eliminating or minimizing distractions

In today's world, minimizing distractions is critical to staying productive and focused. Some effective strategies include turning off notifications on phones and email, avoiding social media during work hours, and keeping the workspace free from clutter. Having a clear mind and distraction-free workspace can help maintain focus and boost productivity.

5. Time-saving techniques for routine tasks

Tasks like answering emails, phone calls, and attending meetings are essential but can take up a large chunk of a workday. Time-saving techniques, like batch tasking, can be beneficial. Group similar tasks together to save time and enhance efficiency. For instance, schedule time for email responses or attend all meetings in a block to maximize productivity.

6. Maximizing productivity during high-energy periods

Most people have energy and productivity peaks. They should identify their high-energy periods and plan tasks that require high levels of concentration and focus. Scheduling peak energy tasks during these times ensures better decision-making and efficient use of time.

In conclusion, productivity is critical in today's world, and effective time management is the key to success. Simple strategies like setting deadlines and delegating tasks, minimizing distractions, and maximizing high-energy periods can make a significant difference in improving productivity. By using these effective techniques, we can create more efficient and productive days that leave us feeling accomplished.

CHAPTER 5: MANAGING TIME FOR WORK-LIFE BALANCE

Many people struggle with the balancing act between work and personal life, often feeling like they are stretched too thin and not able to give enough attention to either. In today's fast-paced world, it can be difficult to maintain a healthy work-life balance. However, managing time effectively is crucial to achieving this balance. In this chapter, we will explore strategies for managing time that will help you prioritize your personal life and create a more fulfilling lifestyle.

Importance of Work-Life Balance in Time Management

In today's society, there is a constant push towards working longer hours, with many people feeling the need to be available 24/7. This can result in burnout and negatively impact your personal life, leading to stress, anxiety, and decreased satisfaction.

It's essential to recognize that your personal life is just as crucial as your professional life, and both require time and attention. Failure to prioritize your personal life can lead to lower levels of satisfaction in both areas and leave you feeling overwhelmed.

Strategies for Balancing Work and Personal Life

❖   Schedule personal time: Just as you schedule work-related tasks and meetings, it's essential to schedule personal time. This can include anything from exercising, reading a book, or spending time with family and friends. Block out specific times in your calendar and make them non-negotiable.

❖   Set boundaries: The ability to set boundaries is crucial to achieving a work-life balance. Learn how to say no to tasks that will interfere with your personal life, and don't feel guilty for doing so. It's also essential to set boundaries within the workplace. Consider setting designated office hours and avoid checking work-related emails after-hours.

❖   Prioritize self-care: Self-care is often neglected in our hectic lives, but it's essential for maintaining a healthy work-life balance. Make time for activities that make you feel good, such as meditation, yoga or mindfulness practices. Take breaks throughout the day to recharge, and don't forget the importance of a good night's sleep.

❖   Delegate tasks: Learn to delegate tasks that can be done by others. Whether it's at work or home, delegating tasks can help free up time for you to focus on more important responsibilities or simply take some time for yourself.

❖   Unplug: In today's hyper-connected world, it's essential to unplug and disconnect regularly. Set aside time each day to disconnect from technology and enjoy some uninterrupted personal time.

Importance of Self-Care in Time Management and Productivity

Self-care is essential because it can directly impact your productivity, allowing you to work more efficiently, accomplish more, and feel more fulfilled. When you take care of yourself, you're better equipped to handle the challenges of daily life.

Strategies for Managing Stress and Maintaining a Healthy

Work-Life Balance

❖ Exercise: Exercise is an effective way to manage stress, improve mood, and increase energy levels. Incorporate physical activity into your daily routine, whether it's a quick walk during the day, a yoga class, or a trip to the gym.

❖ Prioritize sleep: Sleep is essential for overall health and productivity. Make sure to get the recommended amount of sleep each night, and don't underestimate the power of a quick nap during the day.

❖ Practice mindfulness: Mindfulness involves paying attention to the present moment and can be an effective stress management technique. Incorporate mindfulness practices into your daily routine, such as meditation or breathing exercises.

❖ Take breaks: Taking short breaks throughout the day can help keep you focused and energized. Consider taking a quick walk, stretching, or taking a few minutes to chat with a colleague.

Balancing Multiple Roles and Responsibilities

Balancing multiple roles and responsibilities can be challenging, but it's important to find ways to manage your time effectively. Whether you're a parent, spouse, or caregiver, it's essential to prioritize your responsibilities, communicate effectively, and set boundaries.

❖ Prioritize responsibilities: Determine what responsibilities are most important and prioritize them accordingly. This may mean delegating certain tasks or being selective about which activities you participate in.

❖ Communicate effectively: Communication is critical when balancing multiple roles and responsibilities. Make sure to communicate your needs and boundaries effectively to those around you.

❖   Set boundaries: Set boundaries for work-related activities that may interfere with family or personal life. Consider setting designated work hours or avoiding work-related tasks during specific times of the day.

Conclusion

Achieving a healthy work-life balance is essential for overall well-being and satisfaction in both personal and professional life. By managing time effectively, you can prioritize your personal life and create a more fulfilling lifestyle. Strategies for managing stress and maintaining a healthy work-life balance include prioritizing personal time, setting boundaries, prioritizing self-care, and balancing multiple roles and responsibilities. Remember, by taking care of yourself, you're better equipped to handle the challenges of daily life.

CHAPTER 6: OVERCOMING PROCRASTINATION

Procrastination is a major obstacle to effective time management. It is the act of delaying or putting off tasks that require immediate attention or require more work or effort. It is a common problem affecting people of all ages and professions, and it can have serious consequences on productivity, performance, and overall quality of life. However, overcoming procrastination is not impossible. With effective time management strategies, it is possible to turn procrastination into a productive force.

Defining Procrastination

Procrastination is a common problem that affects people in various ways. For some, it is the act of delaying work or tasks until the last minute, while for others, it is a continuous cycle of delaying work or tasks until it becomes overwhelming. Regardless of the context, procrastination can lead to stress, anxiety, and poor health.

Causes of Procrastination

The causes of procrastination are numerous and varied. It can be triggered by a lack of motivation, fear of failure, perfectionism, lack of direction, lack of interest, or difficulty concentrating.

It can also be caused by external factors such as distractions, overwhelming workload, pressure from others, or unexpected events. To overcome procrastination, it is essential to identify the underlying causes.

Strategies for Overcoming Procrastination

1. Create a Sense of Urgency

One effective way to overcome procrastination is to create a sense of urgency. This involves setting deadlines for tasks and breaking them down into smaller, manageable parts. By creating a sense of urgency, you will be motivated to work more efficiently and to prioritize your work.

2. Use Positive Self-Talk

Procrastination is often the result of negative self-talk or the belief that you are not capable of completing a task. To overcome procrastination, use positive self-talk to motivate and inspire you. Remind yourself of your strengths and abilities and celebrate small victories as you progress towards achieving your goals.

3. Avoid Multitasking

Another strategy for overcoming procrastination is to avoid multitasking. Multitasking can be overwhelming and lead to stress and anxiety. Instead, focus on one task at a time, and give it your full attention. This will help you to complete each task more efficiently and reduce the likelihood of procrastination.

4. Use Time Management Techniques

Effective time management techniques such as daily schedules and prioritization can help to overcome procrastination. By creating a daily schedule, you can plan your tasks for the day and prioritize them based on their importance and urgency. This will help you to stay focused and motivated while reducing the likelihood of procrastination.

5. Embrace Procrastination

While it may seem counterintuitive, embracing procrastination can help to overcome it. By understanding the causes of procrastination, you can learn to manage it more effectively. Accept that procrastination is a natural part of the creative process and use it to your advantage by taking short breaks to refresh your mind and refocus your attention.

Conclusion

Overcoming procrastination is essential for effective time management. By understanding the causes of procrastination and using effective strategies to manage it, you can turn procrastination into a productive force. Use positive self-talk, avoid multitasking, use time management techniques, embrace procrastination, and celebrate small victories as you progress towards achieving your goals. With these strategies, you can achieve greater productivity, performance, and overall quality of life.

CHAPTER 7: ELIMINATING TIME WASTERS

Time wasters are the bane of good time management. Even the most organized and focused individual can easily lose track of time when confronted with these distractions. In this chapter, we will look at common time wasters and how to avoid them, as well as time-saving techniques and tools.

Email and Social Media

Email and social media are without a doubt some of the largest culprits of time wasting. According to a study, the average worker spends nearly a quarter of their workday dealing with emails alone. Combine this with social media and suddenly, even the most efficient worker can find themselves mired in a web of distractions.

So how can one eliminate these time wasters? One solution is to set aside specific time periods for checking emails and social media. When you're not in one of these time periods, close your email tab and put your phone in another room. This can help you focus on your work and avoid distractions.

Another solution is to utilize software such as Freedom or RescueTime that allows you to block specific websites or applications during certain times of the day. This can be particularly helpful if you find yourself gravitating toward social media or non-work-related websites when you should be focusing on work.

Multitasking

While it might seem like multitasking would help you get more done in a shorter amount of time, it actually has the opposite effect. Studies have shown that multitasking can actually decrease productivity by up to 40%. This is because each time you shift your focus from one task to another, it takes your brain a few minutes to readjust, which can eat up valuable time.

To avoid multitasking, try to focus on one task at a time. If you find yourself getting bored or restless, take a quick break to recharge your energy before moving onto the next task.

Meetings

Meetings can be both necessary and helpful, but they can also eat up valuable time if not managed properly. To make meetings more productive, schedule them for a specific amount of time and stick to that timeframe. This helps ensure that the meeting doesn't drag on longer than it needs to and keeps everyone focused.

Additionally, make sure that the meeting has a clear agenda and goals that are communicated beforehand. This allows everyone to come to the meeting prepared and ready to discuss the topics at hand.

Traveling/Commuting

Traveling or commuting to and from work can also be a time waster if not utilized properly. One solution is to use this time for personal or professional development activities such as listening to podcasts or audiobooks. This can help you learn something new or stay current on industry trends without sacrificing time that could be spent getting other work done.

Another solution is to use this time to plan for your day or week ahead. This can help you feel more organized and prepared for the tasks at hand, making you more productive when you arrive at your destination.

Energy Drains

Energy drains are anything that Depletes your energy levels. For example, engaging in activities that you don't particularly enjoy or doing work that is demotivating. This not only makes it harder for you to complete tasks effectively but can also lead to burnout and decreased productivity.

One solution is to schedule your day in a way that allows you to tackle the tasks that you enjoy or that energize you in the morning when you have the most energy. This can help you get these tasks done more quickly and with less effort, freeing up more time and energy for other tasks.

Another solution is to take frequent breaks to recharge your energy levels throughout the day. This can involve taking a short walk, doing some light stretching, or simply stepping away from your desk for a few minutes to clear your head.

Saying "No"

One of the easiest ways to eliminate a time waster is simply to say "no" to non-essential activities or requests. This can be difficult in some situations but learning to prioritize your time and say no, when necessary, can help you avoid getting bogged down in non-essential tasks or activities.

Time-Saving Tools and Resources

There are many time-saving tools and resources that can help you eliminate time wasters and boost your productivity. One such tool is a time tracking app like Toggl or RescueTime, which can help you see where your time is going and identify areas for improvement.

Another useful resource is the Pomodoro technique, which involves breaking your workday into 25-minute intervals with short breaks in between. This can help you stay focused and energized throughout the day.

Finally, consider utilizing time-saving resources like virtual assistants or automation tools for tasks that are time-consuming or repetitive. Outsourcing non-essential tasks can free up valuable time and energy for more important tasks.

Conclusion

Eliminating time wasters is crucial for effective time management. By identifying and avoiding common time wasters like email and social media, multitasking, and unproductive meetings, you can free up valuable time and boost your productivity. Additionally, utilizing time-saving tools and resources can help streamline your workflow and make better use of your time.

CHAPTER 8: TIME MANAGEMENT FOR GOAL ACHIEVEMENT

Introduction

Time management, in essence, is the practice of allocating your time effectively to complete tasks and achieve goals. The importance of setting goals cannot be overstated in time management. Setting clear goals makes it easier to prioritize tasks and allocate time to activities that help achieve those goals. Effective time management involves identifying goals, breaking them into smaller tasks or milestones, and allocating time effectively to complete each task. This chapter delves into the importance of goal setting in time management, strategies for setting and achieving goals, and time management tools and resources to achieve your objectives.

Importance of Goal Setting in Time Management

Goal setting is integral to effective time management. Setting goals helps identify the tasks that contribute to achieving those goals, and prioritizing these activities based on their relation to achieving the objectives. While some might see setting goals as a daunting task, it is much easier when approached systematically. First, identify the larger goal or objective you wish to achieve. It could be a big project, a target revenue figure, a promotion, or a healthier lifestyle. Next, break the larger goal into smaller, more manageable milestones. This will help you track progress and see how the smaller tasks that contribute to the bigger objective fall into place. Identify deadlines for each milestone or task to hold yourself accountable.

Strategies for Setting and Achieving Goals

❖ Be Specific: When setting goals, be as specific as possible. Clearly outlining what your goal is, why you're setting it and what you aim to achieve from it, helps bring clarity to the task ahead.

❖ Make them Measurable: Identifying clear and quantifiable metrics for your goal helps track progress and measure achievement.

❖ Set Achievable Objectives: While it is great to aim high and set ambitious goals, ensure they are achievable. Setting unrealistic objectives can lead to frustration, demotivation, and ultimately, failure.

❖ Keep them Relevant: Align your goals with your passions and purpose. This will help maintain motivation and stay on track.

❖ Set Deadlines and Stick to them: Establish deadlines for each task or milestone and stick to them. Establish time frames for achieving each deadline, and work towards meeting each of them.

❖ Use the SMART (Specific, Measurable, Achievable, Relevant, Time-bound) Framework: The SMART Framework is a popular tool used in effective goal-setting, and it can help establish clear and effective benchmarks towards achieving your goals.

❖ Reward Yourself: Celebrate each milestone and task completion. Treat yourself as a way to maintain motivation and keep pushing towards achieving your larger objectives.

Time Management Tools and Resources for Goal Achievement

❖ Trello is a task management tool that allows you to organize goals and tasks in a visual and engaging way. It is a great tool to plan and prioritize tasks in a way that makes sense for you.

❖ Todoist helps you track progress through the lifecycle of achieving your goals. It allows you to allocate tasks, time for completion, and prioritize activities. It also allows for integration with other tools and platforms.

❖ Google Calendar is a widely used tool to track appointments, meetings and deadlines, and allocate time for your tasks. It also allows for scheduling reminders, so you are never caught off-guard.

❖ Focus@Will is a music service designed to improve focus and concentration. When you sign up for the service, you can choose from a set of background music options that will help you focus better and complete tasks more efficiently.

❖ Wunderlist is a to-do list app that makes it easier to manage tasks and maintain focus on goals. It allows for setting deadlines, reminders, and prioritizing tasks.

❖ RescueTime is a tool that helps track your activity online and offline. It provides insights into how you spend your time, helping identify areas that need to be improved and allocated appropriately towards achieving your goals.

Conclusion

Effective time management involves much more than just ticking items off your to-do list. It is the practice of allocating your time effectively, especially towards activities that help you achieve your goals. Establishing clear goals makes it easier to prioritize tasks, allocate time effectively, and measure progress towards your objectives. Breaking down larger goals into smaller tasks, and setting deadlines holds us accountable, and helps us track our progress. Numerous time-management tools and resources exist to help us achieve our objectives. These resources can be adapted to different contexts as we strive towards perfection, continuous improvement, and personal and professional development.

CHAPTER 9: MANAGING TIME FOR PERSONAL DEVELOPMENT

One of the most rewarding and fulfilling aspects of time management is setting aside time for personal development. Personal development can mean different things to different individuals, but it generally includes activities that enable growth, learning, and the building of skills outside of the realm of work or personal relationships. From learning a new language to taking up a new hobby, personal development can be an incredibly fulfilling and enjoyable pursuit.

Setting aside time for personal development can be challenging, particularly for individuals who lead busy lives or have numerous professional or personal responsibilities. However, with the right strategies and mindset, it's possible to make personal development a priority and integrate it seamlessly into our routines.

Importance of Personal Development in Time Management

In addition to being a fulfilling pursuit, personal development can also contribute to overall productivity and effectiveness. By learning new skills or building on existing ones, individuals can become more efficient, organized, and effective in both their personal and professional lives.

Moreover, personal development can also contribute to overall well-being and mental health. By engaging in activities that bring joy and satisfaction, individuals can reduce stress, boost mood, and improve overall quality of life. This, in turn, can lead to increased productivity and effectiveness in other areas of life.

Strategies for Finding Time for Personal Development

Finding time for personal development can be challenging, but by employing the following strategies, individuals can make personal development a manageable and fulfilling pursuit.

- ❖ Prioritize Personal Development: First and foremost, it's crucial to make personal development a priority. This means carving out dedicated time in one's schedule for pursuing personal goals and interests. By treating personal development as an important part of one's routine, individuals can avoid the trap of neglecting this essential aspect of personal fulfillment and growth.

- ❖ Create a Routine: Developing a routine for personal development can be highly effective in ensuring consistency and commitment. Whether it's setting aside an hour each day for language learning or dedicating a weekend morning to taking up a new hobby, creating a routine can help make personal development a seamless part of one's week.

- ❖ Integrate Personal Development with Other Activities: Another effective way to make time for personal development is to integrate it into other activities. For example, if an individual enjoys walking in nature, they may choose to listen to an audiobook or podcast that allows for learning or skill-building while enjoying the outdoors.

❖   Take Small Steps: Personal development goals can seem overwhelming, particularly if they involve learning a new skill or diving into a new hobby. However, by breaking down larger goals into smaller, more manageable steps, individuals can make progress without becoming overwhelmed. For example, an individual interested in writing may start by committing to writing a single page or paragraph each day, gradually building up to a larger project.

Importance of Self-Reflection and Self-Awareness in Personal Development

Self-reflection and self-awareness are critical components of personal development. Without an understanding of one's strengths, weaknesses, and areas for improvement, it can be challenging to set meaningful and achievable personal development goals.

Self-reflection and self-awareness involve taking time to reflect on one's thoughts, feelings, and behaviors, as well as seeking feedback from others. This practice can help individuals identify areas for growth, as well as develop a deeper understanding of their passions and interests.

Strategies for Tracking Progress and Setting New Goals

Tracking progress and setting new goals are essential components of ongoing personal development. By monitoring progress and setting achievable goals, individuals can maintain momentum and continue to grow and develop over time.

Some effective strategies for tracking progress and setting new goals include:

❖   Keeping a personal development journal to track progress, thoughts, and ideas

❖ Setting SMART goals (specific, measurable, attainable, relevant, and time-bound)

❖ Celebrating successes and reflecting on areas for growth

❖ Seeking feedback from mentors or trusted advisors

❖ Integrating new skills or knowledge into daily life or work routines

Balancing Personal Development with Other Responsibilities

While personal development is an essential component of personal fulfillment and growth, it's important to balance personal development with other responsibilities and obligations. This means ensuring that personal development pursuits do not interfere with work or personal relationships and setting realistic expectations for progress and growth.

Furthermore, it's important to remember that personal development should be enjoyable and rewarding, rather than a source of stress or pressure. By maintaining a healthy balance between personal development and other responsibilities, individuals can enjoy the benefits of personal growth and fulfillment while maintaining overall well-being and productivity.

Conclusion

Personal development is an essential aspect of personal fulfillment and growth, and by incorporating personal development strategies into one's schedule and routine, individuals can maximize productivity and effectiveness while maintaining overall well-being. Through self-reflection and goal-setting, individuals can identify their areas for growth, and by setting meaningful and achievable goals, they can continue to grow and develop over time. While balancing personal development with other responsibilities can be challenging, by prioritizing personal development and maintaining a healthy balance, individuals can enjoy the benefits of personal growth and fulfillment while maintaining overall productivity and effectiveness.

CHAPTER 10: TIME MANAGEMENT FOR EFFECTIVE COMMUNICATION

Effective communication is one of the most important skills required for effective time management. In a world of fast-paced business and personal relationships, we are bombarded with multiple channels of communication, including social media, email, text messages, instant messaging, and phone calls, to name a few. In today's globalized and virtual environments, we need to not only manage our time effectively but also manage our communication efficiently. In this chapter, we will explore some strategies and tips for managing communication channels and technologies, prioritizing messages, and responding to them efficiently.

Strategies for managing communication channels and technologies

The first step in managing communication channels and technologies is to evaluate the effectiveness of each channel and device. Do not use all communication channels available to you just because they exist. Instead, evaluate which ones you need keeping in mind the nature of your job and responsibilities.

For instance, if you prefer using email as a form of communication, try and reduce the number of email services you use and stick with one primary email address. This helps you capture all your email correspondence in one place. An important tip to remember is to label your emails and messages to help with sorting responses. Additionally, you can use filters to categorize promotional or irrelevant emails.

Tips for prioritizing messages

One of the most effective ways to prioritize messages is by setting specific time slots for responding to messages. For instance, set specific times during the day when you will check your email, voicemail, and other messaging applications. This way, you will not be interrupted by every message or notification that comes through.

Another effective tip is to use a "one-touch" approach to messages. Do not open messages until you are ready to respond to them. If opening messages distracts you, consider putting your phone on silent or turn off your email notifications for a period of time. Alternatively, you can use color-coded labels for various types of messages, which helps you prioritize them.

Techniques for organizing and prioritizing communication

Organizing your communications is an important part of effective time management. Here are some tips for organizing your communications:

- ❖ Create folders to store messages by category and importance.

- ❖ Colour code messages based on their priority level.

- ❖ Use tags, labels, and filters to sort and manage emails.

- ❖ Prioritize messages based on deadlines, urgency, and

importance.

❖ Use a project management system to manage communication with teams and stakeholders.

The role of active listening in effective communication and time management

Active listening is a crucial skill in all forms of communication. It involves being fully present and engaged with the person you are communicating with and providing feedback to ensure that the message has been received accurately. Active listening is especially important in virtual communications, where visual cues may be absent or difficult to interpret.

To practice active listening, make sure you are fully present during each communication and that you ask clarifying questions to ensure that you understand the message. If you are having difficulty understanding the message, repeat what you have heard back to the speaker to ensure clarity.

Strategies for managing difficult conversations and conflicts

Difficult conversations are an inevitable part of communication, and often need to be managed effectively to avoid confrontation or conflict. Here are some strategies for managing difficult conversations:

❖ Plan and prepare for the conversation in advance.

❖ Remain calm, professional, and empathetic throughout the conversation.

❖ Maintain eye contact and engaged body language.

❖ Use active listening techniques to ensure accurate understanding.

❖ Avoid being defensive or judgemental; focus on finding

solutions to the problem instead of blaming others.

❖ Take a break if necessary to give yourself and the other party time to reflect on the conversation.

Time-saving tips for communication activities

The following are time-saving tips for communication activities:

❖ Use templates for common messages and responses.

❖ Create shortcuts for frequently used phrases.

❖ Use a dictation software or voice-to-text feature for faster messaging.

❖ Set up automatic responses for frequently asked questions.

❖ Schedule email and message replies to be sent during off-hours when you are not working.

The importance of clear and concise communication in time management

Finally, it is important to communicate in a clear and concise way to save time and avoid misunderstandings. To communicate clearly:

❖ Use precise language and avoid technical jargon.

❖ Get to the point quickly and avoid rambling or unnecessary details.

❖ Use bullet points or lists for easy-to-digest information.

❖ Leave out unnecessary information that may confuse the message.

In conclusion, managing communication channels and technologies, prioritizing messages, and responding to them efficiently are critical skills for effective time management. Effective communication is about providing and receiving information in a way that is clear and effective. By practicing active listening, organizing communication activities, and using time-saving techniques, we can communicate more effectively and save time for other important activities.

CHAPTER 11: MANAGING TIME IN A TEAM ENVIRONMENT

Effective teamwork requires the coordination of multiple individuals striving towards a common goal. Despite everyone's intentions, it's typical for team members to have varying degrees of strengths or weaknesses when it comes to time management. This is why effective team time management is vital for optimum productivity. In this chapter, we'll explore some strategies for managing time in a team environment.

Strategies for Managing Time in a Team Environment

1. Clear Communication

An effective time management team starts with clear communication. Each team member must clearly understand their roles and responsibilities. If the objective is not established clearly, team members might feel demotivated and confused. When developing a project timeline, ensure every member comprehends their tasks and how to contribute to the project.

2. Time-Saving Technology

Technologies like instant messaging apps, web conferencing, and project management software are great tools for team communication and collaboration. Use technology to communicate, collaborate, and share information to reduce delays associated with waiting to meet in person.

3. Effective Planning

Collaborative planning is necessary for effective team time management. Plan with the team, set the goals, estimate the resources required, allocate responsibilities, establish timelines, and deadlines. Collaborate on schedules and deadlines that work for everyone. Allow enough padding in tight schedules to offset anything unexpected.

4. Delegation

Delegate tasks and responsibilities smartly in order to bring out the best in each team member. By doing this you're promoting self-development, minimizing time wastage and enhancing productivity. Distribute the workload equally based on each member's strengths and weaknesses.

5. Combatting Procrastination

Procrastination can easily occur in a team environment. Encouraging team members to mentally prepare for projects as soon as they are assigned can go a long way. By doing this, members can prioritize the project in their minds, making it easier to tackle when the time comes.

6. Monitoring Progress

Monitoring and evaluating progress is another strategy for effective team time management. Team members should provide progress updates regularly to ensure that the project is on track, and everyone is aware of the status. This can be done through meetings, check-ins or sending regular updates.

7. Clearing the Pathway for Collaboration

Collaboration is the key to effective team time management. Put down the barriers to collaboration and allow team members to work together without unnecessary hindrances. This can include open communication, avoiding undermining, and promoting collaboration and cooperation.

8. Celebrating Milestones

Finally, throughout the project timeline, it's good to celebrate milestones along the way as a team. Recognize individual team member contributions to the project and how it will collectively impact the final outcome. Celebrating the success thus far will motivate team members to continue working hard.

Managing time in a team environment can be complicated, as it involves managing different personalities, priorities, and working styles. However, by following the above tips, you'll be well on your way to effective team time management. Remember, communication, clear planning, delegation, and recognition, are the hallmarks of a time-effective team.

CHAPTER 12: TIME MANAGEMENT FOR EFFECTIVE DECISION MAKING

Every day, we make countless decisions, ranging from the trivial to the life-changing. In our personal and professional lives, the quality of our decisions can have a significant impact on our success and happiness. However, with so many choices and competing demands for our time and attention, decision making can become a source of stress and overwhelm. In this chapter, we explore strategies for making effective decisions in a timely manner, so that we can maximize our productivity and achieve our goals.

Importance of Effective Decision Making in Time Management

Effective decision making is essential for efficient time management because it helps us to:

- ❖ Prioritize tasks based on their importance and urgency

- ❖ Avoid unnecessary delays and indecision

- ❖ Minimize the risk of making costly mistakes or missed opportunities

- ❖ Allocate our time and resources effectively

❖ Make progress towards our goals and objectives

Strategies for Making Effective Decisions

The following are some strategies for making effective decisions and managing our time:

1. Gather and Analyze Information

Before making a decision, it is important to gather and analyze as much relevant information as possible. This may involve researching options, talking to experts or colleagues, or reviewing data and statistics. It is important to keep an open mind and be willing to consider different perspectives and sources of information.

To avoid getting bogged down in information overload, it is important to focus on the most relevant and reliable sources, and to organize the information in a way that makes it easy to compare and evaluate.

2. Evaluate Options and Choose the Best Course of Action

Once we have gathered and analyzed the relevant information, it is time to evaluate the options and choose the best course of action. This may involve weighing the pros and cons of each option, assessing the risks and benefits, and considering our values and priorities.

To make this process more efficient, we can use decision-making tools such as decision matrices or SWOT analysis. These can help us to compare and prioritize options based on different criteria, such as cost, feasibility, impact, or alignment with our goals.

3. Use Intuition and Gut Instincts

While it is important to use data and analysis to inform our decisions, our intuition and gut instincts can also play a valuable role. These internal sources of guidance can help us to tap into our subconscious knowledge and experience, and to identify options that may not be immediately apparent.

To use intuition and gut instincts effectively, it is important to cultivate awareness and mindfulness, so that we can identify and trust our inner signals. This may involve practices such as meditation, journaling, or simply taking time to reflect before making a decision.

4. Manage Uncertainty and Risk

Making decisions always involves some degree of uncertainty and risk. To manage these factors effectively, it is important to:

- ❖ Anticipate potential risks and outcomes

- ❖ Plan for contingencies and worst-case scenarios

- ❖ Identify and mitigate any biases or assumptions that may cloud our judgment

- ❖ Seek input and feedback from others, especially those with different perspectives or expertise

- ❖ Embrace uncertainty as an opportunity for learning and growth

5. Celebrate Progress and Learn From Decisions

Finally, it is important to celebrate progress and learn from our decisions, whether they are successful or not. This can help us to:

- ❖ Build confidence and motivation

- ❖ Refine our decision-making process and strategies

- ❖ Adapt to changing circumstances and feedback

❖ Recognize and appreciate the value of our time and efforts

Conclusion

Effective decision making is a critical component of time management and can help us to achieve our goals and live fulfilling lives. By gathering and analyzing information, evaluating options, using intuition, managing uncertainty, and learning from decisions, we can make decisions efficiently and effectively. By doing so, we can optimize our use of time and resources, and create the life we desire.

CHAPTER 13: TIME MANAGEMENT FOR LEADERSHIP

As a leader, time management is critical for your success. You are not only responsible for managing your own time but also for leading and managing the time of your team. Your team looks up to you for guidance on how to manage their time and complete their tasks efficiently. Below are some strategies that can help you manage your time as a leader:

❖ Prioritize Your Responsibilities: As a leader, you are responsible for several tasks, so it's essential to prioritize your responsibilities. Use the Eisenhower Matrix to categorize tasks into urgent and important and assign them according to their due dates and their impact on your organization. Prioritizing your tasks will help you stay on top of your responsibilities and accomplish your most critical tasks first.

❖ Delegate Tasks: Delegating tasks is also crucial for time management. You can increase your efficiency and productivity by assigning tasks to your team members based on their strengths and weaknesses. By delegating, you can devote your time to strategic planning and other critical leadership responsibilities.

❖ Manage Expectations: It's easy to become overwhelmed

as a leader, so it's essential to manage expectations. Set realistic timelines for tasks and let your team know about the timelines. This will help you avoid last-minute crises and stress. You can also manage expectations by communicating clearly and effectively with your team members.

❖ Lead by Example: As a leader, your actions set the tone for your team. If you're not managing your time effectively, your team members won't do so either. Therefore, it's vital to lead by example and show your team members how to manage their time efficiently.

❖ Coach Your Team: Coaching is an essential aspect of leadership, and it can also help improve time management skills. Offer coaching and mentoring to your team members to help them improve their time management skills. By coaching them, you can help them work efficiently and strategically, and provide them with the tools they need to improve their time management skills.

❖ Focus on Strategic Planning: As a leader, your role is to plan, set goals and formulate strategies for your team. You must spend dedicated time on strategic planning so that your team can work effectively and efficiently towards these goals. By focusing on strategic planning, you can provide direction to your team, and ensure that your team is always working towards critical business goals.

❖ Take Care of Yourself: As a leader, it's easy to neglect self-care in favor of work and other responsibilities. However, self-care is essential for maintaining your energy levels and keeping you motivated and engaged. Take time every day to do something that rejuvenates you and helps you relax, such as meditation, exercise, or reading a book. This can help you stay on top of your leadership responsibilities and ensure that you are energized and motivated consistently.

❖ Use Time Management Tools: Technology can be a powerful tool for time management, and there are various tools available that can help you manage your time effectively. Use these tools to automate routine tasks, manage your calendar, and prioritize your to-do list. Gain insights from data by using time tracking software to understand where your time is being spent, and how you might improve your approach to managing your time.

Leadership time management may be challenging when your priorities are pulled in different directions, but effective management of your time can make all the difference in your success. By prioritizing your tasks, delegating, managing expectations, leading by example, and taking care of yourself, you can successfully leverage your time and guide your team to greater levels of productivity and success.

CHAPTER 14: TIME MANAGEMENT FOR ENTREPRENEURS

Time management is a crucial aspect of entrepreneurship, and it can make all the difference between a successful business and a failed one. Entrepreneurs often face unique challenges and opportunities when it comes to time management, from managing a fast-paced environment to balancing work and personal life. This chapter will explore strategies and tips for managing time and priorities as an entrepreneur.

One of the most significant challenges entrepreneurs face when it comes to time management is balancing multiple responsibilities. Entrepreneurs often must handle several crucial tasks simultaneously, from developing new products to marketing and sales activities. To overcome this challenge, entrepreneurs must learn to prioritize their tasks and focus on the most important ones at any given time. One useful technique is to identify the tasks that are most critical to the success of the business and tackle them first. Entrepreneurs should also work on delegating tasks as much as possible to maximize their time and efficiency.

Staying focused and avoiding distractions is also essential for entrepreneurs. Entrepreneurs must learn to manage their time and energy effectively to avoid wasting precious resources on non-essential tasks or activities. One technique is to develop a routine and stick to it consistently. Entrepreneurs should set aside specific times during the day for crucial tasks and avoid any distractions during those times. For example, setting aside specific times for checking email or social media can help entrepreneurs stay focused on critical tasks.

Another critical aspect of time management for entrepreneurs is prioritizing business development and growth activities. Entrepreneurs must be willing to spend time and resources on developing new products or services and expanding their customer base. This requires careful planning and execution, as well as a willingness to take calculated risks. Entrepreneurs should be willing to experiment with new ideas and techniques, but they should also be willing to pivot quickly if an approach isn't working.

Another key strategy for time management as an entrepreneur is outsourcing and delegating tasks. Entrepreneurs often face a never-ending list of tasks and responsibilities, which can quickly become overwhelming. By outsourcing some of these tasks to external contractors or delegating them to team members, entrepreneurs can free up time and energy to focus on more critical activities. This can also help entrepreneurs to develop their leadership skills and empower team members to take ownership of their work.

Maintaining work-life balance is also critical for entrepreneurs when it comes to time management. Entrepreneurs can easily fall into the trap of working around the clock, neglecting their personal and family lives. This can lead to burnout and compromised mental health, making it difficult to sustain the long-term growth of the business. Entrepreneurs should identify personal and family priorities and ensure they are dedicating enough time to them. By prioritizing self-care and family time, entrepreneurs can maintain the energy and focus needed to succeed in their business.

Lastly, entrepreneurs must learn to celebrate their successes and learn from their failures. Entrepreneurship is a continuous process that requires ongoing learning and experimentation, and entrepreneurs must be willing to learn from their experiences. This means celebrating their achievements and recognizing the progress they have made, as well as taking note of failures and using them as learning experiences. By adopting a growth mindset and continuously seeking to improve, entrepreneurs can leverage their time and resources effectively to grow their businesses.

In conclusion, time management is an essential aspect of entrepreneurship that can make all the difference in the success and growth of a business. By focusing on prioritization, focus, growth, delegation, work-life balance, and learning from failures and successes, entrepreneurs can optimize their time and maximize their productivity, leading to long-term success and growth.

CHAPTER 15: MANAGING TIME DURING TRANSITION

Transitions are a natural part of life, and they can be both exciting and stressful. Whether it is transitioning to a new job, moving to a new city, or starting a new phase of life, transitions require adjustments to routines, priorities, and goals. Effective time management during transition can be the key to a smooth and successful transition.

Strategies for managing time during transitions and change:

1. Create a Transition Plan

One of the first steps during a transition is to create a plan. This plan should consider both the old and new routines and priorities. Transition plans can help establish a roadmap to follow and provide structure to the process.

2. Set Realistic Expectations

Transition periods can be overwhelming, and it is important to set realistic expectations. Setting unachievable goals can result in disappointment and frustration. Break goals down into smaller, achievable steps and prioritize those that are most important.

3. Assess the New Environment

During a transition, one needs to learn new routines, environments, and cultures. This can take time, so assessing the new environment and determining how the transition will affect daily and long-term schedules is essential.

4. Stay Organized

Transition periods can be chaotic, but maintaining organization is key. Effective time management relies on organization. Staying organized can help prevent confusion, stress, and potential setbacks.

5. Stay Focused

Transitions can be a distraction to long-term goals and priorities. To prevent this from happening, it is important to stay focused on the long-term goals and to keep the overall end-point in mind.

6. Remain Flexible

Transitions are not always smooth, and there can be unforeseen obstacles. It is important to remain flexible and adaptable to changes. Having flexibility in the plan can help manage stress and offer new opportunities.

7. Embrace Change

Transitions offer new and exciting opportunities. Embracing change can offer a fresh perspective and new possibilities. An optimistic outlook can help manage stress and foster growth.

8. Self-Care

Transitions can be stressful, so self-care is essential during this time. Taking care of oneself, both physically and mentally, can help prevent burnout and exhaustion.

Transitions can be a time of growth and opportunity, but they can also be stressful and challenging. Effective time management can help ease the transition process, increase productivity, and reduce stress. By creating a transition plan, setting realistic expectations, staying organized, staying focused and flexible, embracing change, and practicing self-care, one can manage time during the transition successfully.

CHAPTER 16: TIME MANAGEMENT FOR CONTINUOUS IMPROVEMENT

While it's crucial to create a time management plan that works for you, it's equally important to keep improving and refining it. Continuous improvement is key to achieving long-term success with time management.

Continuous improvement is the process of identifying areas for improvement and continuously making changes to enhance and refine outcomes. Time management is no different. Once you have a time management plan that works, it's essential to find ways to improve upon it and ensure that it stays effective.

Here are some strategies and tips for achieving continuous improvement in time management:

Identify Areas for Improvement

The first step towards continuous improvement in time management is identifying areas that can be improved. Self-reflection is crucial here. You need to assess your time management habits and habits to find areas that require improvement.

Some potential areas for improvement include productivity during specific times of the day, dealing with distractions, and managing priorities. Look for areas where you struggle to stick to your time management plan or where you could be achieving more.

Set New Goals and Track Progress

Once you have identified areas for improvement, the next step is to set new goals and track your progress towards achieving them. This will keep you accountable and enable you to see how effective your new strategies are.

When setting goals, start small, and don't be too hard on yourself. For example, if you struggle to stick to your morning routine, maybe your goal could be to stick to it for three consecutive days. When you've achieved that goal, set the next one.

Experiment with New Strategies and Tools

Continuous improvement in time management also means trying out new strategies and tools to see if they work better for you. Keep a journal and make a note of what works and what doesn't. Plan their use for specific situations too.

For example, if you're struggling with distractions during the day, try using the Pomodoro technique where you work for 25 minutes and then take a 5-minute break, each time wasting 1 pomodoro. If it works, great. If it doesn't, keep trying out other tactics till you are successful.

The Role of Self-Awareness and Feedback

Self-awareness is crucial when it comes to continuous improvement in time management. You need to be aware of your strengths and weaknesses to find areas that need improvement.

Ask for feedback from those around you, too, to find where you can improve. Your coworkers, friends, and family may have ideas on where you could make improvements that you might not have thought of.

Celebrate Progress and Small Wins

Lastly, it is essential to celebrate progress and small wins along the way. This helps you stay positive and motivated to make changes and continuously improve.

Every small goal achieved is a cause for celebration. So, take a moment to enjoy what you've accomplished. This helps you be more focused and committed towards the next goal.

Continuous improvement is essential in time management. Implementing the strategies above can help you create an excellent time management plan that you continuously enhance and refine. Remember to be patient, stay disciplined, and embrace the rewards that come with regularly improving your time management skills.

CHAPTER 17: TIME MANAGEMENT FOR GLOBALIZATION

In our ever-changing world, globalization has become a prominent feature of business. With businesses expanding their reach beyond borders, time management has encountered its own set of complexities. Managing time with colleagues and clients in other time zones can lead to fatigue and burnout. So, how do we manage our time effectively in a globalized world?

The first step to managing time in a globalized world is to familiarize yourself with different time zones. It is important to be aware of the current time and date in the time zone where your colleagues and clients are located. You can also save different time zones on your calendar so that you don't have to keep converting the time every time you schedule a meeting.

Communication is key to effective time management in a globalized world. It is essential to have clear communication with your colleagues and clients. You should clarify the expectations and establish a routine for regular check-ins. With different time zones, it is important to schedule meetings at a convenient time for all parties involved. This means that you may have to stretch your working hours or start earlier to accommodate for the time difference.

To maximize productivity in a globalized world, you should also consider leveraging technology. There are a few apps available that can help to manage time effectively. For example, World Clock provides real-time clock for different time zones worldwide, and Google Calendar allows recipients to modify the time zone for a specific event.

When the work hours extend beyond the normal working hours, you should also take care of your personal well-being. It is important to take some time for self-care and maintain a balanced lifestyle to prevent burnout and stress. Exercise, meditation, and rest are all effective ways of rejuvenating your mind and body.

Lastly, you should embrace cultural differences and diversity in a globalized world. Appreciating the cultural norms of your colleagues and clients is essential to building healthy and productive working relationships. Take the time to learn about different cultures so that you can understand and communicate effectively with others.

In conclusion, managing time effectively in a globalized world can be challenging, but it is possible with the right strategy in place. Familiarizing yourself with different time zones, clear communication, leveraging technology, prioritizing personal well-being, and embracing cultural differences can all contribute to for effective time management in globalization. By mastering the skills of time management in a globalized world, you can thrive in a fast-paced, international business environment.

CHAPTER 18: TIME MANAGEMENT FOR RETIREMENT

Retirement is a time in life that many people look forward to with anticipation. After years of hard work and dedication, retirement offers the opportunity to relax, explore new interests and hobbies, and spend time with loved ones. However, retirement also comes with its own unique challenges, including how to manage time effectively. In this chapter, we will explore the various time management strategies and tools that can help retirees make the most out of their newfound freedom.

One of the biggest adjustments in retirement is transitioning from a structured daily routine to a more open-ended schedule. With no set work hours or deadlines, it can be tempting to take a more laid-back approach to time management. However, without structure, it can be easy to fall into a trap of boredom and inactivity. Therefore, it's important to create a new routine that allows retirees to stay active and engaged.

One strategy is to establish a daily or weekly schedule that includes both leisure activities and personal development or growth opportunities. For example, retirees can set aside time for exercise, hobbies, volunteering, or learning something new. Having a planned schedule provides structure to the day, helps maintain productivity, and allows retirees to make the most out of their limited time.

It's also important to set realistic goals and expectations for retirement. Retirement provides more time for relaxation and exploring new interests, but it's important to have a purpose and meaning behind these activities. Setting goals and objectives can help retirees stay motivated and enhance their sense of fulfillment. Goals can be related to personal development, family, health, or career aspirations. Regardless of the goal, having a purpose can help retirees stay engaged and make the most of their retirement years.

Another challenge in retirement can be the financial constraints that often come with a fixed income. However, this limitation can also force retirees to be smart with their time management. For example, retirees can save money by cooking at home, walking or biking instead of driving, and taking advantage of senior discounts. These time-saving practices can help to make the most out of a fixed income and provide more flexibility in how to spend that limited budget.

Retirement is also a time for retirees to focus on their health and well-being. With more time and flexibility, retirees can prioritize their self-care needs. This includes regular physical activity, healthy eating, and sufficient sleep. Incorporating these healthy habits into a daily schedule can help retirees maintain their physical and emotional health and enhance their overall happiness.

It's also important to stay socially connected during retirement. Many retirees experience feelings of isolation or loneliness after transitioning from a busy work environment to a more isolated lifestyle. To combat this, retirees should seek out social activities and maintain their relationships with loved ones. This may include joining community organizations or clubs, volunteering, or attending social events. Maintaining social connections can help retirees stay active, engaged, and fulfilled during retirement.

Finally, it's important for retirees to embrace the freedom and opportunities that come with retirement. Retirement is a unique opportunity to pursue new interests, create new relationships, and live life to the fullest. It's an excellent time to explore hobbies, travel to new places, and spend quality time with family and loved ones. By embracing the full range of opportunities that retirement offers, retirees can make the most of their time and experience a fulfilling and satisfying retirement.

In conclusion, retirement provides a unique opportunity to explore new interests, embrace freedom, and make the most of life. However, effective time management is crucial for retirees to maintain productivity, prioritize self-care, and enjoy all that retirement has to offer. By establishing a meaningful daily routine, setting goals and objectives, staying socially connected, and practicing healthy habits, retirees can enhance their sense of satisfaction, purpose, and fulfillment in retirement.

CHAPTER 19:
CONCLUSION:
THE ART OF TIME
MANAGEMENT
FOR LIFE

Time is not only one of the most precious commodities we have, but also the most elusive. It slips away from us when we're not paying attention, leaving us with a sense of unease and anxiety as deadlines loom and tasks pile up. However, with the right approach and mindset, it is possible to master and harness time to achieve our personal and professional goals.

Throughout this book, we've explored different aspects of time management, from understanding your personal time management style to creating a time management plan, and from overcoming procrastination to managing time in a team environment. We've discussed the importance of work-life balance, effective communication, and continuous improvement. Now it's time to bring it all together and consider how the art of time management can benefit us in all areas of our lives.

First and foremost, time management is about setting priorities and achieving goals. When we manage our time effectively, we are able to focus on the tasks that are most important and meaningful to us, while setting aside distractions and energy drains that don't contribute to our success. This means approaching each day with intention, purpose, and a clear plan of action.

Time management is also about striking a balance between productivity and self-care, work and life, personal goals and professional responsibilities. By taking care of ourselves physically and emotionally, we have the energy and motivation to achieve our goals. By investing in our personal growth and development, we become better equipped to succeed in our chosen fields.

Effective time management also requires self-awareness, reflection, and continuous improvement. By monitoring our habits and behavior, we can identify areas where we need to improve and experiment with new approaches to time management. By learning from our successes and failures, we can refine our strategies over time.

Finally, effective time management requires tools and resources that support our goals and style. Whether it's using a calendar app to manage our schedule or a productivity tool to streamline our work, we need tools that work for us, not against us. The right tools can help us save time, reach our goals more efficiently, and give us the structure we need to thrive.

In conclusion, the art of time management is not just about managing minutes and hours; it is a way of life. By mastering time management, we unlock the potential to achieve our personal and professional goals, become more productive and less overwhelmed, and find greater balance and fulfillment in all areas of our lives. The journey to effective time management may take time, patience, and effort, but the rewards are well worth it. So let's embark on this journey together and experience the impact of better time management on our lives.

CHAPTER 20: RESOURCES AND TOOLS FOR TIME MANAGEMENT

Effective time management is a journey, rather than a destination, and it requires continuous learning, exploration, and experimentation. In this final chapter, we will take a closer look at some of the resources and tools that can help you master the art of time management for life.

Overview of Time Management Resources and Tools Covered in the Book

Throughout this book, we have explored numerous time management resources and tools that can help you boost productivity, achieve your goals, and achieve a healthy work-life balance. Here is a brief overview of some of the most important resources and tools we have covered:

❖ Time Management Apps: Time management apps are designed to help you track your time, manage your tasks, set reminders, and prioritize your activities. Some of the most popular time management apps include Trello, Todoist, RescueTime, and Asana.

❖ Productivity Tools: Productivity tools can help you

streamline your work processes, reduce distractions, and stay focused. Some popular productivity tools include Evernote, Pocket, and Grammarly.

❖ Goal Setting and Planning Tools: Goal setting and planning tools can help you set SMART goals, create action plans, and monitor your progress. Some popular goal setting and planning tools include MindMeister, Wunderlist, and Toggl.

❖ Communication Tools: Communication tools can help you stay in touch with team members and clients, track your emails and messages, and communicate effectively in a globalized world. Some popular communication tools include Slack, Zoom, and Google Hangouts.

❖ Self-Care Apps: Self-care apps can help you manage stress, promote relaxation, and support your mental health and well-being. Some popular self-care apps include Headspace, Calm, and YogaGlo.

Additional Time Management Resources and Tools for Ongoing Success

The world of time management is constantly evolving, and there are countless resources and tools that can help you stay on top of your game. Here are some additional resources and tools that can support your ongoing success:

❖ Online Courses: Many online courses are available on topics such as time management, productivity, leadership, communication, and personal development. Some popular websites that offer online courses include Coursera, Udemy, and LinkedIn Learning.

❖ Books: There are countless books on time management that can help you continue to learn and grow. Some popular books include The 7 Habits of Highly Effective People by Stephen Covey, Getting Things Done by David Allen, and

Atomic Habits by James Clear.

❖ Podcasts: Podcasts can provide a wealth of knowledge and inspiration on topics related to time management, productivity, goal setting, personal development, and leadership. Some popular podcasts include The Tim Ferriss Show, The Productivity Show, and Optimal Living Daily.

❖ Coaching: Working with a time management coach can help you set goals, create action plans, and stay accountable for your progress. Many coaches specialize in time management, productivity, and leadership.

Tips for Selecting and Using Time Management Resources and Tools Effectively

While there are many resources and tools available for time management, it's important to choose the right ones for your needs and goals. Here are some tips for selecting and using time management resources and tools effectively:

❖ Start with your goals: Before selecting a time management tool or resource, it's important to clarify your goals and objectives. What are you hoping to achieve with your time management efforts?

❖ Do your research: Take time to research different time management tools and resources before investing in them. Read reviews, watch demos, and ask for recommendations.

❖ Test before committing: Many time management tools offer free trials or introductory periods. Take advantage of these opportunities to test the tool before committing to a subscription or purchase.

❖ Integrate with your existing systems: The best time management tools should be able to integrate with your existing systems, such as your calendar, email, and task list.

❖ Keep it simple: Time management tools should be easy to use and integrate into your daily routine. Avoid tools that are overly complicated or require significant training.

❖ Stay flexible: Remember that your time management needs will change over time, and you may need to adjust your tools and resources accordingly.

Suggestions for Creating a Personalized Time Management Toolkit

Building a personalized time management toolkit can help you stay focused, organized, and on track. Here are some suggestions for creating a personalized toolkit that works for you:

❖ Start with your goals: As with selecting resources and tools, it's important to start with your goals. Identify the tools and resources that will help you achieve your specific goals.

❖ Keep it simple: Your time management toolkit should be simple and easy to use. Avoid using too many tools or resources, as this can lead to overwhelm and confusion.

❖ Integrate with your existing systems: Your time management toolkit should integrate with your existing systems, such as your calendar, email, and task list.

❖ Set reminders and notifications: Use alerts, notifications, and reminders to keep yourself on track and accountable.

❖ Regularly evaluate and adjust: Your time management needs and goals will change over time, and it's important to regularly evaluate and adjust your time management toolkit accordingly.

Importance of Ongoing Learning and Exploration in Time Management

Finally, it's important to remember that time management is an ongoing process of learning, exploration, and experimentation. The more you learn about time management, the more effective you will become at maximizing productivity, achieving your goals, and finding a healthy work-life balance. Make learning and exploration a priority in your time management efforts and stay curious and open to new ideas and strategies.

In conclusion, mastering the art of time management requires ongoing learning, exploration, and experimentation. By selecting the right resources and tools, creating a personalized time management toolkit, and staying open to new ideas and strategies, you can achieve your personal and professional goals, while maintaining a healthy work-life balance. Remember, effective time management is not about being perfect, but about continuously striving to improve and grow.

Final Thoughts

I hope this book has given you valuable insights and practical strategies to take control of your time and achieve your goals. Remember that time management is not about squeezing more tasks into your day or working harder, but about being intentional and strategic in how you use your time.

As you implement the techniques outlined in this book, don't forget to be flexible and adapt them to your personal circumstances. What works for one person may not work for another, so take the time to experiment and find what works best for you.

Finally, always remember that time is a finite resource, but how we choose to spend it ultimately determines our success and happiness. So make every moment count, prioritize what truly matters, and don't be afraid to say no to distractions that take away from your goals.

Thank you for taking the time to read The Art of Time Management. My hope is that you have found value in these pages and that it has helped transform the way you think about and utilize your time. Here's to a more productive and fulfilling life!

ABOUT THE AUTHOR

Ray Goodwin

Ray Goodwin, is the author behind this series of captivating books on Business Development and self improvement, and has left an indelible mark on the field. He was born and raised in the bustling city of London, where he developed a strong work ethic and an insatiable curiosity about the inner workings of successful businesses. Throughout his illustrious career, Ray leveraged his extensive knowledge and experience to help numerous companies flourish and prosper.

His keen insights and innovative strategies has earned him recognition, driving him to share his expertise with others. Ray believes in the power of sharing knowledge to elevate businesses and empower aspiring entrepreneurs.

Ray's dedication to his craft is evident in the numerous books he has authored on business development and self improvement. His writing style seamlessly blends practical advice, thought-provoking concepts, and real-life case studies, making his books invaluable resources for business professionals and novices alike. His ability to distill complex concepts into accessible language has greatly impacted the lives and careers of countless individuals.

Now retired from the corporate world, Ray and his beloved wife have settled in the idyllic English countryside. Surrounded by the beauty of nature, Ray finds inspiration for his writing and indulges in his hobbies.

Ray Goodwin's books continue to serve as enduring guides for those seeking success in the business world. With a wealth of experience and a deep understanding of the inner workings of businesses, Ray's work remains a testament to his passion for sharing knowledge and helping others flourish.